# ————CONTE

## CHOICE

Sarah Howe • *Foretokens* • Chatto & Windus

## RECOMMENDATIONS

Troy Cabida • *Neon Manila* • Nine Arches Press
John F. Deane • *Jonah and Me* • Carcanet Press
Lena Khalaf Tuffaha • *Something About Living* • The 87 Press
Joelle Taylor • *Maryville* • Bloomsbury

## SPECIAL COMMENDATION

Salena Godden • *With Love, Grief and Fury* • Canongate

## TRANSLATION CHOICE

Phoebe Giannisi • *Goatsong* • Translated by Brian Sneeden • Fitzcarraldo

## PAMPHLET CHOICE

Helena Fornells Nadal • *I Could Not Ask You To* • Mouse Press

# Poetry Book Society

| | |
|---|---|
| CHOICE SELECTORS<br>RECOMMENDATION<br>SPECIAL COMMENDATION | YOMI ṢODE<br>& VICTORIA KENNEFICK |
| TRANSLATION SELECTOR | SHIVANEE RAMLOCHAN |
| PAMPHLET SELECTORS | YOUSIF M. QASMIYEH<br>& ALYCIA PIRMOHAMED |
| CONTRIBUTORS | MEGAN ROBSON<br>THE WRITING SQUAD<br>THE YOUNG POETS SUMMIT |
| EDITORIAL & DESIGN | ALICE KATE MULLEN |

**Poetry Book Society Memberships**

**Choice**

**4 Books a Year:** 4 Choice books & 4 *Bulletins* (UK £65, Europe £85, ROW £120)

**World Poetry**

**8 Books:** 4 Choices, 4 Translation books & 4 *Bulletins* (£98, £160, £190)

**Complete**

**24 Books:** 4 Choices, 16 Recommendations, 4 Translations & 4 *Bulletins* (£230, £290, £360)

**Single copies of the *Bulletin*** £12.99

**Cover Artwork:** Victo Ngai Instagram: @victongai

Supported using public funding by
**ARTS COUNCIL
ENGLAND**

MIX
Paper | Supporting
responsible forestry
FSC® C014866

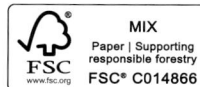

Poetry Book Society | Milburn House | Dean Street | Newcastle upon Tyne | NE1 1LF
0191 230 8100 | enquiries@poetrybooksociety.co.uk

WWW.POETRYBOOKS.CO.UK

# LETTER FROM THE PBS

A warm welcome to our Winter *Bulletin*! It's a pleasure to reach out to our readers directly after nine years as Poetry Book Society Manager. It's been a labour of love redesigning the *Bulletin*, immersing myself in the selections and typesetting each word (every line break matters). It's often a welcome anchor, in the whirlwind of managing the PBS, to return to the poetry and people at the heart of it. Recently the poet Lisa Kiew sent us a parcel of archive issues from the 1950s-70s and it struck me, more than ever, that we're carrying forward such a vital poetry legacy. We're delighted to welcome Emily Keeling as the new Managing Director of Inpress and the Poetry Book Society. With over a decade of experience with the company and a deep understanding of its operations she's well placed to lead this new chapter.

Next year will mark our 10th anniversary in Newcastle and we're looking to the next generation. In this issue we've joined forces with The Young Poets Summit and The Writing Squad to offer talented young poets the opportunity to review. While we're rooted in Newcastle, we have a truly global outlook. In recent years we've represented UK poetry in Beijing and Jaipur and showcased poets from Bhutan, Switzerland and India at Newcastle Poetry Festival. We really are nurturing a global poetry community from our tiny Newcastle office. It's been so lovely to welcome new members from Canada to New Zealand at our online showcases. If you missed the Winter Showcase, you can catch up on the Member's Area.

Our brilliant Selectors continue to open our eyes to new possibilities in poetry. The Winter Selections span the small-but-mighty new Mouse Press to the first book in a decade by T.S. Eliot prize winner, Sarah Howe. Huge thanks to our cover artist, the LA based Hong Kong illustrator Victo Ngai, whose contemporary take on traditional Chinese ink art, like Sarah Howe's poetry, leaps across time and continents. Our PBS Recommendations include rising star Troy Cabida on queer Filipino experiences and a powerful voice from the Palestinian diaspora, Lena Khalaf Tuffaha. Poetry Ireland's Founder John F. Deane stills busy brains with his ability to hold a moment; former T.S. Eliot Prize winner Joelle Taylor reclaims lost LGBTQ voices and Salena Godden reminds us "that whatever divides us, our humanity must never be forgotten". These are poems of furious hope and, in an increasingly divided world, we need them more than ever.

In this spirit of empathy and connection, poetry makes the perfect gift and our Christmas catalogue is full of ideas to share the joy of poetry. For a truly thoughtful gift, treat someone special to a Gift Membership and a year of inspiring poetry. Every Gift Membership, book sale and donation helps us support the poetry community. Merry Christmas to our fellow poetry fans and heartfelt thanks.

ALICE KATE MULLEN, PBS MANAGER

# MEET THE SELECTORS

## BOOKS

Victoria Kennefick: "In dark times it can seem that light is an impossibility – but it is when we enter these shadowy places courageously and in search of the truth that we realise that light is inevitable. Poetry can be that light. These Poetry Book Society Selections are the light. Allow them to shine for you."

Yomi Ṣode: "The last 12 months as Selector have been a pleasure. My appreciation for my fellow Book Selector, Victoria is beyond measure. I am grateful for her thoughts, humour and the many moments we explored these collections, wishing we could add them all. The Winter Selections range through themes of identity, love and culture, but most importantly for me, a feeling of communion; the collective action needed for change and awareness raising."

## TRANSLATION

Shivanee Ramlochan: "Language is what we have: sometimes it's the only thing we can offer each other, across borders, over cultural and political divides. The gift of reading so many poetry books in translation has been an extraordinary one. I'll never stop being grateful to The Poetry Book Society for the privilege."

## PAMPHLETS

Born and educated in Baddawi refugee camp in Lebanon, Yousif M. Qasmiyeh is a poet and translator with a doctorate in English Literature from the University of Oxford. His debut *Writing the Camp* (Broken Sleep Books) was a 2021 PBS Recommendation and his latest book is *Eating the Archive* (Broken Sleep Books). He edits *Migration and Society* journal and is Writer-in-Residence for the Refugee Hosts project.

Alycia Pirmohamed is the author of *Another Way to Split Water*, *Hinge*, *Faces that Fled the Wind*, and *Second Memory* with Pratyusha. Her nonfiction debut *A Beautiful and Vital Place* won the 2023 Nan Shepherd Prize. Alycia teaches on the Creative Writing master's at the University of Cambridge, and she is the co-founder of the Scottish BPOC Writers Network.

# MEET OUR YOUNG REVIEWERS

MEMORY BHUNU is a Zimbabwean-born poet. A Verve Poetry Collective member, they won Unislam and headlined at Birmingham Festival. Their pamphlet *Memory Flowers* was published by Fawn Press and they cohost Pretty Privilege Poetry.

SETH CONNOR-FULLWOOD is a writer, performer, facilitator, and editor from Manchester. His poems have been published in Young Identity's *An Island Under Water*, *Creation Through From*, *The Bread and Roses Poetry Award Anthology 2024*, *Manchester Memories: A Triumph Over Adversity,* and *The AVE* Issue #1.

BETH DAVIES is the Sheffield Poet Laureate. She won the 2022 New Poets Prize and her pamphlet *The Pretence of Understanding* was published by The Poetry Business.

JASMINE GRAY is a Northern writer published in *Anthropocene*, *The London Magazine*, and *The Double Negative*. She has published two pamphlets *Let's Photograph Girls Enjoying Life* (2019) and *Open Your Mouth* (2023).

KAYLEIGH JAYSHREE is a poet and Roundhouse Collective alumna who has performed at Glastonbury Festival. Her pamphlet is due out with fourteen poems.

GREGORY KEARNS is a writer based in Liverpool. He has been published in *Bath Magg*, *The Mersey Review* and *Not About Now*. He has worked with English Heritage and No Dice Collective and hosts The Poems We Made Along The Way podcast.

ALEXIA McPHERSON is a 22 year old queer artist specialising in drag and spoken word. Alexia contributed to ORIGIN, a sound exhibition at Dunham Massey.

JAY MITRA is a British Indian punk poet, non-fiction writer and educator from Yorkshire, currently based in London. They are a Roundhouse Poetry Collective alum and a T.S. Eliot Prize Young Critic. Find them on social media @punkofcolour.

PÈLÚMI OBASAJU is a Nigerian-British poet. She was part of the Poetry Translation Centre's UNDERTOW cohort, and The Southbank Centre New Poets Collective 23/24 and has been commissioned by the London Philharmonic Orchestra and Lagos International Poetry Festival. Her self-published pamphlet *Love LETTERS & HEART Ramblings* debuted at number 3 on Amazon Christian Poetry.

ANZAL OMAR is a poet with a background in aerospace engineering. Her work appeared in *After Hours* (Hive, 2023) and she performed at Migration Matters.

LEON RAY-FERNANDES is a Barbican Young Poets alumnus based in London.

AARIB ZAMAN is a member of Young Identity and has performed across the UK.

# SARAH HOWE

Sarah Howe is a British poet, academic and editor. Born in Hong Kong to an English father and Chinese mother, she moved to England as a child. Her pamphlet *A Certain Chinese Encyclopedia* won an Eric Gregory Award, and her first collection *Loop of Jade* (Chatto & Windus, 2015) won the T.S. Eliot Prize and the *Sunday Times* Young Writer of the Year Award, and was shortlisted for the Forward Prize for Best First Collection. In 2014, she co-founded *Prac Crit*, an online journal of poetry and criticism. She is currently the Poetry Editor at Chatto & Windus and an Honorary Visiting Professor at the University of Liverpool.

# FORETOKENS

CHATTO & WINDUS        |        £12.99        |        PBS PRICE £9.75

FORETOKENS

SARAH HOWE

*Foretokens* are premonitory shadows, the future visiting the now, a brilliantly resonant organising principle which not only echoes through Sarah Howe's eagerly-awaited second collection but also chimes with her T.S. Eliot prize-winning debut *Loop of Jade,* which explored her dual Chinese British heritage and her complex relationship with her mother. Now a mother herself, Howe's perspective in navigating the knotty inheritance of family, language and colonialism has shifted and deepened with time. *Foretokens* is also a portrait of a mother in search of her past and herself. In the opening poem 'Calendar' there is an immediate representation of the effects of migration on the speaker's mother, "Unearthed in a clear-out, a picture calendar she's kept / – hoarding, I've learnt, is a mark of the emigrant". The poet unpacks and catalogues an intimate history through objects, which are part of her story too: "How quaint it seems, my birth-year, or how colonial: / *Birthday of Her Majesty* sits days from *Tuen Ng Festival.*"

Poems like 'Waking' and 'Songs Spun of Us', early in the collection are lyrical, physical and, in 'Undersong 1's case, almost concrete exemplars of the strata that Howe as poet is called on to curate and excavate – the connections between generations of mothers and daughters, between belonging and not, life and death: "o mums  mo urn / o  u  no urn." These compelling dynamics are revealed in a contested domestic arena in the unforgettable 'A History of My Relationship with my Mother in Twenty-three Arguments about the Laundry' where the mother-daughter boundaries are laid bare in "adventures in passive aggressive laundry."

The standout poems, among many, carry a deep awareness of place, lineage and history as earthenware objects of witness share their stories, such as 'Finely Potted White Glazed Porcelain Cup, Dehua Ware' which succinctly predicts, "The English will forget who invented tea." The poem is a receptacle, then a thread, imitating the molecular structure of DNA, a "ladder of atoms beginning to twist". Both raw materials (clay and DNA) mould and spiral to manifest the tangible, biological, physical world. This paradoxically gives rise to the astonishing final sequence, 'An Error, A Ghost' suggesting, as in the epigraph by Jorge Luis Borges, the eternal labyrinthine nature of existence. *Foretokens* elegantly holds this existential contradiction, "Pity those who make their mothers / into myths – for them is reserved a special kind of hell – /...and overlapping, are the others, / the ones who must make their myths into mothers."

8        VICTORIA KENNEFICK

# SARAH HOWE

I try to hold in mind the almost exactly ten-year span between the publication of my first book of poems *Loop of Jade* and my second, *Foretokens*. I find myself unable to grasp that unwieldy chunk of living, to try to give it shape, navigable landmarks: in those ten years, my son was born, my daughter was born; my nephew died, my father died. In those ten years, I mostly wrote no poems, until I did. And then the poems began to pour out like one of those sudden, thrilling rain showers that sluice the windscreen of your car till you can't see a thing and have to pull off the road.

*Foretokens* opens with a series of poems dredged from the depths of early motherhood: a voice pieced together from the fragments of a former self. I felt like I had to learn again from scratch how to construct a poem, as if from first principles – any accumulated experience or skill having gone out the window. For the most part, the poems are rangier, messier, less controlled than those of *Loop of Jade*. After a long period of silence, I felt myself slowly letting down my guard. Unguarded is a good word for these poems. Becoming a mother – and more particularly, moving back into my parents' house after our first baby was born – I found myself impelled to revisit my own mothering with new eyes, and with it the long shadow of intergenerational trauma.

A central spine of poems takes the molecular structure of DNA as its template, a "ladder of atoms beginning to twist", down which I found myself stepping into the darkness of deep time. What unfolds is a personal Babel of voices and identities, and an examination of the contradictory legacies of colonialism, where poems – past and present – act as "foretokens", omens of what lies ahead.

## SARAH RECOMMENDS

These books helped me find my way as I worked: Karen Downs-Barton, *Minx* (Chatto); Sandeep Parmar, *Faust* (Shearsman); Ed Bok Lee, *Mitochondrial Night* (Coffee House Press); Paul Tran, *All the Flowers Kneeling* (Penguin); Victoria Chang, *Obit* (Corsair); Monica Youn, *From From* (Carcanet); Ocean Vuong, *Time is a Mother* (Cape); Hannah Sullivan, *Was It For This* (Faber); Mary Jean Chan, *Bright Fear* (Faber); Carl Phillips, *Scattered Snows, to the North* (Carcanet); Jorie Graham, *To 2040* (Carcanet); Kit Fan, *The Ink Cloud Reader* (Carcanet).

I CHOICE

# PORCELAIN TEA CADDY PAINTED IN UNDERGLAZE BLUE

Far blue peaks retreating into memory
as wizened cedars twist against a glaze

of sky... these whimsical scenes so finely
brushed across my surface resemble

nothing I've seen on my crossings. I watch
this latest well-heeled young gent press his suit

as they practise their pouring, the lily-
fingered daughters of the prosperous

Liverpool merchant who spotted me buried
on a stall of fans and girdles. A seafarer

come good, still he has an eye: a man
of taste, my owner. His girls will have all

the graces, proficient in the rituals
around this steaming, still-exotic brew

that measures out an empire's domain
while glancing, spout poised, from the corner

of an eye. I observe from my silver tray.
Where do you think it comes from, capital

to fill a townhouse like this? It's not just wares
like me trussed as cargo. Human beings are,

were always, things. You don't want to see?
He knows, my man of taste. Ask the sugar

bowl here what it is it sweetens. One day
the English will forget who invented tea.

SARAH HOWE

# FORE/MOTHER (EXTRACT)

*Truth becomes fiction when the fiction's true;*
*Real becomes not-real when the unreal's real.*
　　　　– Cao Xueqin, *Dream of the Red Chamber*


What I know begins
outside/within
the limits of Shanghai.
A girl is born, youngest of many.
One day –
if it helps say the bowls are empty –
the girl is
sold to strangers.
If it helps say it sounds like a fairytale.
Did you see the look in her mother's eyes?
This is what happened/happens
then/now
where money buys
desire/silence.
If it helps say her mother was dead.
What she went on to live, what she became
you
can
imagine.

# TROY CABIDA

Troy Cabida is the author of *Symmetric of Bone* (fourteen poems) and *War Dove* (Bad Betty Press). His recent work appears in *State of Play, Bi+ Lines, 100 Queer Poems,* and *Tiffany & Co.*, as well as being shortlisted for the Bridport Prize for Poetry 2024. An alumnus of the Barbican Young Poets, he currently works for the National Poetry Library and holds a BA in Psychosocial Studies from Birkbeck, University of London.

# NEON MANILA

NINE ARCHES PRESS | £11.99 | PBS PRICE £9.00

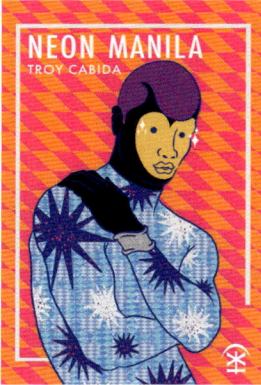

Troy Cabida's *Neon Manila* arrives as the poet's first full collection, yet it feels like the natural culmination of a journey already in motion. His earlier pamphlets *War Dove* (Bad Betty Press, 2020) and *Symmetric of Bone* (Fourteen Poems, 2024) explored themes of wellbeing, queerness, identity, homophobia, urban living and even the quiet power of adornment. With *Neon Manila* these threads gather into something fuller, more assured, as though the earlier books were rehearsals for this deeper reckoning.

What strikes me is how vulnerability is allowed to breathe here. Poetry often becomes the medium where what feels unsayable elsewhere can be witnessed and transformed. Cabida leans into that honesty. The body is a stage within *Neon Manila*, whether clothed in slouchy knitwear or defined by sleek silhouettes. Fashion, in these poems, is never just about clothes but about how we inhabit our own skin, how textures and colours reveal or conceal the self.

> I say I am myself
>
> and you trace me back
> to my all black uniform, my clean,
>
> linear silhouette, so little texture
> distracting from the flesh you say
>
> I look less ethnic now
> compared to that old photograph of myself:
>
> seventeen in mismatched denim, London lights
> glaringly new against my cheeks.

The collection reminds us that identity is always shifting. Cabida asks us to consider what freedom looks like in dress, desire, relationships, and the small gestures of daily life. Reading *Neon Manila* is an invitation to witness a private transformation, not dramatic but steady. It's a reminder that queerness, and individuality can flourish in uncertain times and a collection for anyone who recognises their own body, memory, or longing in these lines. In that sense, the book is more than a collection: it is a spark held up to what it means to become.

YOMI ṢODE

# TROY CABIDA

To me, *Neon Manila* is the light from an exploding flashbulb, the chorus to an infectious Nu-disco pop song, the laugh that comes after sharing yet another sour dating experience with your close friends. It is spraying on that expensive perfume because life is way too long to keep such luxuries from oneself, not caring if the scent isn't at all safe for work.

The poems in this collection are concerned with the cyclical relationship between how a body is approached by those around it, and how this phenomenon might then influence how the self approaches itself. Looking at the modes in which I compose myself interpersonally, sexually, and sartorially, I was initially worried that the objects I wanted to write about wouldn't bear enough weight to be taken seriously as tools to look into one's lived experiences. After taking as much time as I needed to develop the manuscript, I eventually learnt (unsurprisingly) that the political is a multifaceted truth that exists in everything: yes, in the urgent and in the profound, but also in the euphoric and in the insanely ridiculous that leaves you choosing to laugh or else you'll cry. Realising this only pushed me further to finish the book, one that is resolute in its joy, rage, and desire.

If I were to have any goals at all for *Neon Manila*, it would be for it to paint a portrait of a queer Filipino immigrant subjectivity in all of its chronically online humour and fine jewellery sheen. If I could go further, I would even hope that this book would give some level of support to contemporary discourse around the celebration of self as a radical act of love against a system that demands marginalised bodies to embody the opposite.

## TROY RECOMMENDS

Kim Addonizio, *What Is This Thing Called Love* (W.W. Norton & Co); Savannah Brown, *Closer Baby Closer* (Doomsday Press); Wanda Coleman, *Wicked Enchantment* (Penguin); Alex Dimitrov, *Ecstasy* (Penguin); Jameson Fitzpatrick, *Pricks in the Tapestry* (Birds, LLC); Essex Hemphill, *Love is a Dangerous Word: Selected Poems* (New Directions); Joseph Legaspi, *Threshold* (Cavankerry Press); Rachel Long, *My Darling from the Lions* (Picador); Alfonso Manalastas, *A Factory of Alleged Truths* (Ateneo Press); Marilyn Monroe, *Fragments: Poems, Intimate Notes, Letters* (HarperCollins).

I look at people, and they see what they want to see in me

Image: Kulay Labitigan

# BOTH WRISTS SILVERED, WATCH ME DEFLECT

*After Wonder Woman*

teenage boy hate, drunk fathers, slurs
cold like bullets – I started this journey
in satin and gold vermeil, now I fly
in cracked leather and vintage Peretti.
I know this life is grand cinema.
Every part of my outfit is functional,
fashionable for my day job,
flexible enough to push back
the incoming tanks, the groping old men.
Despite all temptations, I've retired my sword,
lasso missiles back to the sky,
walk behind the explosion and smize.
I am all solution, empathy machine
in a boomerang tiara,
comic book scene at high noon,
the one untouchable archetype,
the one you cannot take home
and dismantle.

Image: Moya Nolan

# JOHN F. DEANE

John F. Deane was born on Achill Island, County Mayo, Ireland. He is the founder of Poetry Ireland, the National Poetry Society, and *The Poetry Ireland Review*. He also founded Dedalus Press, of which he was editor from 1985 until 2006. In 2019 he was visiting poet in Notre Dame University, Indiana. His poems have been translated into many languages. Deane is the recipient of numerous awards, a member of Aosdána and was made Chevalier en l'ordre des arts et des lettres by the French Government. His recent books include *Naming of the Bones* (Carcanet, 2021) and *Selected and New Poems* (Carcanet, 2023).

RECOMMENDATION

# JONAH AND ME

CARCANET | £12.99 | PBS PRICE £9.75

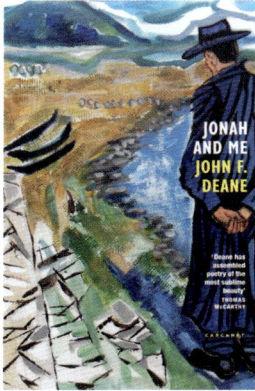

The valley lies still in the profound green
of late summer fullness. Scarcely a breath
on the air. Little expectancy...

'Towards Verse', this gossamer-delicate miniature detailing the experience of the artist in relation to the landscape, opens Deane's latest collection *Jonah and Me*. Nestled in the poem is a beautifully balanced contradiction, the pitch-perfect phrase "little expectancy" which then expands into the realisation, "But the spirit holds". It is this spirit that imbues the poems that follow. Poet as beachcomber in 'Presences,' poet as urban naturalist spy in 'Covert' and as holy man in 'Franciscan Monastery, Achill Island' populate the first section of the book. This section is titled 'For Whom the Bell' in reference to John Donne's 1624 work *Devotions upon Emergent Occasions*, specifically 'Meditation XVII.' In it, the English poet reflects on human interconnectedness, arguing that every peal that signifies the death of another human life, is a toll for each of us.

'Franciscan Monastery, Achill Island' where "you arrive on the verge of prayer, aware how the compassionate / love of our God is extravagant, transcending all belief" makes way for 'Of Human Flesh' a sequence, for several voices, for Holy Week where in the "Rushy Field" it is "time, again, to confess." One of the narrators, a nun, shares her story through the gruelling final penance, replete with real and contemporary horrors, "a child of / Yemen, not yet three, so much of suffering he has no lungs / to scream, the doctors cannot find a vein in that needle-thin / body" pointing to the truth that this child "of human flesh... is all of the children." 'Considering' is a moving selection of poems powerfully exploring that gravestone dash between our birth year and our final one. Poems like 'Midwinter' and 'Between Worlds' lament the passing of loved ones while the speaker pauses with us in the twilight of grief. The collection ends fittingly, and paradoxically in 'Emergence'. Just as we began with "Little expectancy", but considerable "spirit", the final poem wonderfully culminates Deane's project of interrelatedness through the "red bars" of the gate where eventually our spirits:

> may slip out
> through the red gate of the sheepfold, will find
> the longed-for strength – and with a profound sigh
> will soar away towards a long-anticipated rest.

VICTORIA KENNEFICK

# JOHN F. DEANE

I was born and raised on Achill, a wild and ruggedly beautiful island off the west coast of Ireland, a remote place steeped in the old traditions. Roman Catholicism, in its more stringent form, was as natural to me as the rains that came sweeping across the island. I absorbed both the battering and caressing seasons of the Atlantic Ocean, the extended acres of bogland and high heathlands, and was profoundly aware of the poverty of an island where subsistence was difficult: fishing was dangerous, holdings were small, always there were the sorrows of emigration.

Education was limited; I depended on parents and grandparents for wider knowledge and reading. I grew up; life happened; I began to find myself being more encumbered by the rituals of that faith, though still seeking its source and sustenance. Now I seek a more cosmic awareness, a faith more pervious to contemporary actualities. Instead of ingested truths, I see the poet standing like a prophet between the actual and the transcendent, listening, hearing the music of creation, at times its cacophony, at times its symphony, and translating that listening into the music and urgency of words.

I have come to believe that our lives are meshed in Christ, that full-fleshed human being, "ever ancient, ever new", meshed too with all humanity, with the whole of creation, as Darwin presented in *On The Origin of Species*. I would like the poems, too, to probe the idea of the Communion of all humanity and the Darwinian notion of "the tangled bank", and even with the widest notion of Eucharist, in which all of life, all of creation, the cosmos, our common home, all of it is tangled together into an evolving universe, and to bring the strengths of the poetic imagination to bear upon the burdens of our daily living.

## JOHN RECOMMENDS ─────────────

*The Poetry Ireland Review* (www.poetryireland.ie); James Harpur, *The Magic Theatre* (Two Rivers Press); Pádraig J. Daly, *This Glowing Place: New & Selected Poems* (Scotus Press); Moya Cannon, *Bunting's Honey* (Carcanet Press); David Harsent, *Skin* (Faber).

...trust to the day's lightening...

Image: John Behan

# TOWARDS VERSE

The valley lies still in the profound green
of late summer fullness. Scarcely a breath
on the air. Little expectancy. But the spirit
holds. There is much trouble in the world
but no diminution of hope, though the spring
acclamations of birdsong have been falling
silent. Quick mid-summer thunderstorms
have gone by. I have let the red gate swing
open to the demands of noon – in deep
shadows of the wood a smallest creature
stirs, hesitates; at the wood's edge, something
shifts amongst the grasses, falls still. Upstairs
the notebooks lie open, the laptop idles. I
pause a while, inhale, turn towards the house.

# LENA KHALAF TUFFAHA

Lena Khalaf Tuffaha is a poet, essayist and translator. She has published three poetry books: *Something About Living* (University of Akron Press, 2024; The 87 Press, 2025), winner of the 2024 National Book Award for Poetry and the 2022 Akron Poetry Prize; *Kaan & Her Sisters* (Trio House Press), finalist for the 2024 Firecracker Award and honourable mention for the 2024 Arab American Book Award; and *Water & Salt* (Red Hen), winner of the 2018 Washington State Book Award and honourable mention for the 2018 Arab American Book Award. She is also the author of two chapbooks *Arab in Newsland*, winner of the 2016 Two Sylvias Prize, and *Letters from the Interior* (Diode, 2019), finalist for the 2020 Jean Pedrick Chapbook Prize.

# SOMETHING ABOUT LIVING

THE 87 PRESS    |    £16.99    |    PBS PRICE £12.75

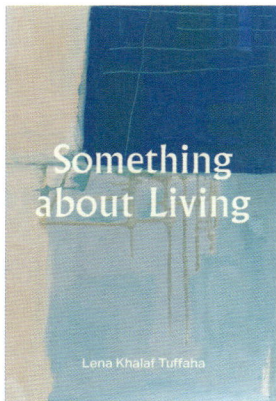

Lena Khalaf Tuffaha's latest collection *Something About Living* arrives at a moment that feels painfully urgent, reminding us why poets of witness, or those who are able to write about lived experiences are crucial in poetry and the overall archiving of literature.

This collection not only speaks of the crimes committed against the Palestinian people. It also carries poems of family and community, an ebb and flow of violence, tenderness, mourning, pain and kindness, rooted in questions of survival, love, and loss. The title, itself, leans on mortality, on what life is worth in another's lens, "The snipers lose interest in shooting at medics evacuating the wounded", and considers ideas of legacy:

> Denuded of my name, of belonging,
> childhood memories grow up in me,
> one day following another.

As in, 'Variations on a Last Chance':

> The fence does not hold.
> The wire sheds its barbs, softens to silk thread.
> The snipers run out of bullets.
> The desert, as it always has, of its volition, blooms.
> The snipers are distracted, sexting their girlfriends.
> The snipers' eyes are blinded by smoke from our burning tires.
> The snipers wonder if they will ever see the end of us.
> The fence does not hold.
> ...
> The bullets disintegrate when they reach the word PRESS on Yasser's vest.

It is important to remember that being alive, particularly when you are Black or a person of colour, is political. It is simply walking into particular spaces, feeling the silent rejection of your presence, of breathing the same air. This pales in comparison to communities waking each morning unsure if they will see the sun rise again.

These poems are gentle, they are a quiet force of storytelling, reminding us that to witness is also to love, to hold one another in our shared humanity.

YOMI ṢODE

SELECTOR'S COMMENT

# LENA KHALAF TUFFAHA

There is a line from a poem by Naomi Shihab Nye scrawled on a notecard and taped above my writing desk: "I begin again with the smallest numbers." I've returned to this line many times; it has become a kind of first breath before I put pen to paper. I think of poetry as a practice of attention. In *Something About Living*, I turn that practice of attention – of close study and of being present – to language.

The Western world generally, and Americans particularly, have a way of talking about Palestinians without naming us, of looking right through us but never actually seeing whole human beings, let alone a people with a homeland and a history. Writing from inside this experience of erasure, all while US foreign policy continues to shape (or more precisely, destroy) Palestinian lives, required the wisdom of Nye's line.

How to find the smallest numbers? The unit of discourse, political and cultural, official and popular, is the word. And so, in these poems, I study the words written about us. I listen for what they say and for what they obfuscate. I trace what ghosts between lines and follow the unspooling of what repeats. I write the echo alongside. And I note the wide swathes of silence that language makes possible.

## LENA RECOMMENDS

Ed. Alan Morrison, *Out of Gaza* (Smokestack Books); Eds. Ahmad Al Naouq and Pam Bailey, *We Are Not Numbers: The Voices of Gaza's Youth* (Penguin); George Abraham and Noor K Hindi, *Heaven Looks Like Us; Palestinian Poetry* (Haymarket Books); Solmaz Sharif, *Customs* (Bloomsbury); Don Mee Choi, *Mirror Nation* (And Other Stories); Sarah Ghazal Ali, *Theophanies* (The 87 Press); Edward Said, *The Question of Palestine* (Fitzcarraldo Editions); Isabella Hammad, *Recognizing the Stranger* (Fern Press).

...Here I should say something about hope. Here I should say something about living.

# THE STATE OF

Noun gerund of the verb (to journey)
A setting out, a departure
A boy's voice calls out from beneath what used to be
the second story of a house
*I am here* he cries *can anyone hear me?*
*I am here and the night sky is sleeping on my chest*

Noun gerund of the verb (to leave)
An exodus, a detachment
A father has gone in search of bread
A baker has gone in search of flour
A mother has gone in search of a cloud
A people have gone
A world in each of them

Noun gerund of the verb (to travel)
A parting, a demise
A girl steps on top of the walls of what used to be
the third story of a house
*I am searching for the sea* she cries
*Has anyone seen it? It used to live in my window.*

Image: Roman Manfredi

# JOELLE TAYLOR

Joelle Taylor is the author of four collections of poetry. Her previous collection *C+NTO & Othered Poems* (The Westbourne Press) won the 2021 T.S. Eliot Prize, and the 2022 Polari Book Prize. She has judged several poetry and literary prizes, including the Forward Prize and the Ondaatje Prize. Taylor is a Royal Society of Literature Fellow and lives in East London.

# MARYVILLE

BLOOMSBURY | £14.99 (HB) | PBS PRICE £11.25

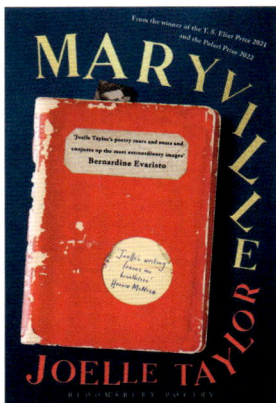

The T.S. Eliot prize-winning poet, Joelle Taylor's electric new collection *Maryville* opens with a dedication to "wrong-walking women" preceding an epigraph from the American poet, essayist and feminist Adrienne Rich, "Courage is not defined by those who fought and did not fall, but by those who fought, fell and rose again." The tangible physicality and inherent sense of movement in both phrases reference the collection's daring and engrossing cinematic aspects. They also serve as a call to arms and a trailer that foreshadows the motion and energy of the poems that follow.

*Maryville* walks us through the lives of four butch dyke friends first introduced in Taylor's outstanding *C+NTO & Othered Poems* her 2021 collection which explored the underground lesbian culture in the 1990s through riotous and lyrical cantos. These recurring characters, listed as in a teleplay by Taylor in the opening pages, enter The Maryville bar in 1957 and remain there until 2007. Taylor describes the collection as being "in the shape of a television series, using the language of film" to guide the reader, to steer their focus through visual and aural techniques. The effect is utterly immersive and interactive – not only because of the structure and visual aspect of the collection and each constituent poem but also because each Mise-en-scène poem has a soundtrack that Taylor suggests the reader listen to as they read.

The experience of reading the combined elements of the book, in addition to the supplementary material that completes it, is deeply moving, culturally and societally significant in terms of Taylor's project, as well as wildly engrossing and entertaining. Jack Catch, the butch bartender in The Maryville is one of the book's brilliantly drawn characters who is also the subject of one of the standout pieces in the collection, including 'Jack: My Body, An Ambush', printed in full on the following pages.

> Jack is framed / within the cell door keyhole / making her a
> woman imprisoned / in the body of a woman

The last line "the rustle of leaving" demonstrates Taylor's unique ability to walk us through the complexities and paradoxes of identity to ultimately capture and champion the lived experience of butch lesbians with fury, skill, deep respect and profound love.

VICTORIA KENNEFICK

# JOELLE TAYLOR

In 2021 I wrote a book called *C+NTO & Othered Poems*, the story of four butch friends and of the forgotten underground dyke scene that once flourished across London. It is a book of hauntings, in which I resurrected the dead and memorialised them, placing them all inside the Maryville dyke bar which in turn is inside a snow globe. Since then, I have been playing more with the idea of ghosts, especially that of the communal ghost, the shared myth, the curation of new legends. I began to wonder what would happen if my friends were not only resurrected but given a different life? What if I could haunt my ghosts?

In *Maryville,* I transplant the characters from *C+NTO* into 1957 when they meet in the dyke bar as teenagers, remaining there for fifty years. It is the story of witness, of resistance, community, and inexorable friendship. Through the Maryville's tinted windows, we can see the shapes of the early Gay Liberation Front forming, holding hands with the Women's Liberation and Black civil rights movements. This is quiet history, archival, the air between us. It seems important to say our names again. It seems important to write.

I use the vocabulary of film within *Maryville* to explore the idea of visibility and presence, of the gaze itself. We zoom in on a tight angle to one poem, pan out into another. Each poem is connected like scenes in a film, and the wider narrative is held together using Mise-en-scène poems – a kind of anamorphic shot of the whole of the Maryville at the start of each decade, or when words are not enough.

After all, what is a film but a haunted house? What is film but the ghosts of who we were yesterday?

## JOELLE RECOMMENDS

Ilya Kaminsky, *Deaf Republic* (Faber); Judy Grahn, *The Common Woman Poems* (Women's Press Collective); Adrienne Rich, *Dream of a Common Language* (Norton); Safiya Kamaria Kinshasa, *Cane, Corn & Gully* (Out-Spoken Press); Malika Booker, Sharon Olds, Warsan Shire, *Modern Poets: Three* (Penguin); Fran Lock, *Hyena! Jackal! Dog!* (Pamenar Press); Gboyega Odubanjo, *Adam* (Faber); K. Patrick, *Three Births* (Granta); Hannah Lavery, *Unwritten Woman* (Polygon); Terrance Hayes, *American Sonnet for My Past & Future Assassin* (Penguin).

RECOMMENDATION

# JACK:
## *MY BODY AN AMBUSH*

Jack is framed / within the cell door keyhole / making her a woman imprisoned / in the body of a woman / a sand timer / she is falling through her own hands / it is true / the crime is the punishment / young jack / holding girls who mistook her for themselves / falling in love like others fall in front of trains / when Elizabeth denied her / three times / she transmuted a kiss under a name / to a wrought iron crucifix / curtsying to men / cassocked as crows / swore Jack was a boy / a charming violence / that she kept her clothes on beneath her skin / that the night is unnatural / that Jack was a fraudster / interloper / thief of the quiet places / thirty pieces of fucking / & now the sun is locked in a metal box / shown to the women / once a day / if you are good / you can hold it / if you are bad / you can hold it / & Jack lays still / listening to night talk / preen the wing / the animal of their mouths / searching for their young / afraid of the soft predator / concealed in the bushes / the rustle of leaving.

# MISE-EN-SCÈNE
## *A MARYVILLE CHRISTMAS* (EXTRACT)

WIDE ANGLE. BACK BAR OF THE MARYVILLE ||

THEY DECORATE THE FAMILY TREE, HANGING TAMPONS SPRAYED IN ANTIQUE GOLD FROM EACH BRANCH, & IMPALING AN EAGLE EYE ACTION MAN ON TOP. DUDZ HAS CUT HIM A TINY LEATHER HARNESS. SOHO SETS A CANDELABRA WITH RED CANDLES ON THE TABLE & LIGHTS HER CIGARETTE OFF IT. A PACKAGE HOLIDAY OF GRINNING FAIRY LIGHTS WAVE THEIR ARMS ACROSS THE BAR. A RAINBOW BEGINS ITS ARC TOWARD THE TABLE, THEN THINKS BETTER OF ITSELF. MUSIC NURSES A PINT, ROCKS & REPEATS ITSELF. JACK CATCH & VALENTINE CARRY FOOD TO THE TABLE. THIS IS THE FEAST OF ST GIRO, THE MARYVILLE TRADITIONAL BUFFET FOR SEASONAL STRAYS...

...

|| CAMERA CHOKER SHOT OF EACH OF THE DINERS ||

THEY SIT DOWN TOGETHER & EAT THEIR FACES, THEIR TROUBLES, THE OVERDUE RENT, THE IMPOSSIBILITY OF LIVING, THE QUALITY OF AIR, HOW THE NIGHT IS NO LONGER QUITE SO NIGHT; THEY SIT TOGETHER & EAT THE YOUNG, THEIR UNENDING DEMONSTRATIONS, THE OBSCENITY ACT, SECTION 28, THEY BRING BOOKS TO THE TABLE ON A LARGE CATERING TROLLEY & DOUSE THEM IN BRANDY. WHEN THEY PULL THE CRACKER THERE IS A TINY PLASTIC SNOWGLOBE INSIDE.

# SALENA GODDEN

Salena Godden FRSL is an award-winning author, poet and broadcaster of mixed Jamaican-Irish heritage. Her debut novel *Mrs Death Misses Death* won the Indie Book Award for Fiction and the People's Book Prize, and was shortlisted for the British Book Awards and the Gordon Burn Prize. Her most recent books include the literary childhood memoir, *Springfield Road* and poetry collections *With Love, Grief and Fury* and *Pessimism is for Lightweights: 30 Pieces of Courage and Resistance*. Her work has been shortlisted for the 4thWrite Short Story Prize, the Ted Hughes Award, Jerwood Compton Foundation, Bridport Poetry Prize and highly commended by the Forward Prize. She is a Fellow of the Royal Society of Literature, a Patron of Hastings Book Festival and an Honorary Fellow of West Dean, Sussex.

# WITH LOVE, GRIEF AND FURY

CANONGATE | £10.99 | PBS PRICE £8.25

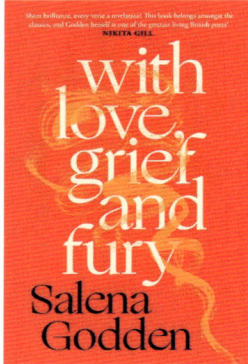

"This is for the poets and provocateurs, the artists and activists, the witches and warriors, the rebels and raconteurs, the full moon lovers and star sailors" claims Salena Godden in this welcoming introduction to her new collection, *With Love, Grief and Fury*.

One of the most fearless and beloved voices in contemporary literature; a writer across genres and a master of performance who brings sparks of energy to the stage in ways that are powerful and tender. Her heart beats loudly for the community. It's as though she has spun the world on its axis with this collection, noting the areas of anguish, the climate, people power and grief.

*With Love, Grief and Fury* urges us, irrespective of race, class or gender to stay awake to the world, its beauty, its pain, its anger, and its resilience. Poems for the unheard that hold truth to power. They do not shy away from anguish or injustice, but within them there is love, wit, and the stubborn pulse of joy. To write and perform with such honesty is an act of bravery. To tell truths that may unsettle is to take on the sacrifice of activism, the knowledge that not every ear will welcome what must be said. This collection is a call to action, a common thread, a shared song, as in her poem 'My Heart is a Boat'.

We're outside a pub
and she's yelling,
telling me to,
*Get back on my boat*

My friends say, *she's just racist*,
but I put down my rum
and walk over and ask,
*Do you need a hug?*

I stand with open arms
as wide as a map of the world,
and she bursts into tears.
I hold her for a while

Salena's poems are for all of us. They are an invitation to remember that whatever divides us, our humanity must never be forgotten.

YOMI ṢODE

# WITH LOVE, GRIEF AND FURY 1

*Summer 2019*

Today Iceland held a funeral
to mourn its first glacier
lost to climate change

the Amazon is on fire
and the black smoke
can be seen from space

the global protests
the world is in flame
everywhere, chaos, conflict

I cannot read this page
my eyes blurred with tears
with love, grief and fury

Image: Onassis Nomos

# PHOEBE GIANNISI

---

# BRIAN SNEEDEN

Phoebe Giannisi is the author of eight collections of poetry. A 2016 Humanities Fellow of Columbia University, Giannisi is a professor of architecture at the University of Thessaly, and co-editor of the literary journal *frmk*. She has translated Ancient Greek lyric poetry as well as the poetry of Barbara Koehler, Gregor Laschen, Jesper Svenbro and André Pieyre de Mandiargues. She lives in Volos, Greece.

Brian Sneeden is the author of *Last City* (Carnegie Mellon, 2018). His poetry and translations have received the Iowa Review Award in Poetry, an NEA Literature Translation Fellowship, the World Literature Today Translation Award for Poetry, the Constantinides Memorial Translation Prize, a PEN/Heim Translation Grant and other recognitions. He is a lecturer in English at Manchester Metropolitan University.

TRANSLATION CHOICE

# GOATSONG
## TRANSLATED BY BRIAN SNEEDEN

FITZCARRALDO     |     £14.99     |     PBS PRICE £11.25

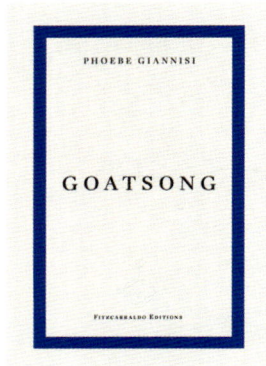

Raise your trumpet high. Herald the goatsong.

Phoebe Giannisi's *Goatsong* gathers three collections: Homerica; Cicada; Chimera, translated from the Greek by Brian Sneeden. These three hundred assembled pages easily – playfully, even – defy any single description, gloriously implicating all manner of living creation, from human narrator to faithful dog to ruminant goat to watchful goatherd, in the act of the poems' creation. The text breathes across its surfaces with such avid curiosity, inviting the reader not only to read, but to immerse wholly in these worlds, these wild, urban, and mythological places.

The host of references and speakers roving through the poems might be dizzying, if they weren't so earnestly and joyously rendered, leaving ample room for interpretation, for the reader's own breath to join the raucous medley. Thetis, "who refused to be assigned / to surrender to a man / becoming / fire wind water / tree chicken tiger / becoming / lion snake cuttlefish", stuns in her transformative ire, her vengeful splendour. John Lennon and Yoko Ono, suspended in the affection of memory as a pair of snapshots, evoke:

> millions of years couples intertwined lying face up couples facing
> the ceiling the sky and lying there.

Goatself, a marriage of the speaker's voice with the embedded voices of all those who occupy a shared space, brings utter polyphonic joy. As Goatself journeys with the Vlach goat herders of Kalamaki Larisis, seeking to understand the ways of these creatures, the poems that emerge owe as much to the animal truth of existence as they do to the human – if not more so. Wisdoms, shorn of artifice, populate the revelations Goatself supplies:

> caring for another saves you
> from your dominant self.

Giannisi's poems, chorusing in their munificence, extend tenderly to us this bleating proposition: that we are better, stranger, beyond our Homo sapiens skins.

SELECTOR'S COMMENT

SHIVANEE RAMLOCHAN

# PATROKLOS II

is it that language follows longing
or is it longing
that's inspired by language?
because Achilles does not accept because you
once rushed to bear arms
Patroklos because
we must since that time rush to recite
the war does not cease at all
a hawk suspended in the sky
the sheep huddled
in the stockyards
you did not hear the airplanes
the washing machine spinning endlessly
and in the fire
the air laden from elsewhere
and singing in the pot
the thyme the savory rosemary
chamomile after being crushed by wheels

# HELENA FORNELLS NADAL

Helena Fornells Nadal is a Catalan poet based in Edinburgh. She is currently engaged in research on the intersection between land politics and ecopoetics. Her work has appeared in publications including *DATABLEED*, *Magma, Gutter, New Writing Scotland, PROTOTYPE* 6 and *Propel. I Could Not Ask You To* is her first solo publication.

# I COULD NOT ASK YOU TO

MOUSE    PRESS                           |                    £8.00              |

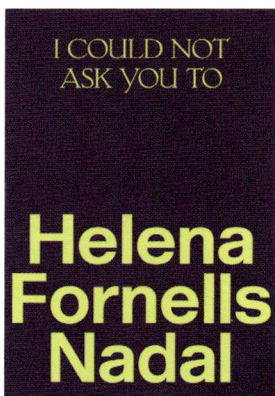

Helena Fornells Nadal's *I Could Not Ask You To* is a complex and searching pamphlet, filled with poems held taut by the poet's charismatic and unique voice. In this work, place – places – are important anchors, and yet slippery still, changing shape as the speaker crosses real and imagined borders. At "dreamy Loch Eck" we are offered a tether in the land: in the loch as a mirror and in the shape of a half-sunken yacht within the water. But for Fornells Nadal, language thrives as a mode of constant transformation, echoing a changing self and her new revelations. What was once clear becomes a cloud – "a second life returned" at the "wrong time", or the stern of a boat dissolving into a stern night.

Thus, these poems feel as if they are in a constantly shifting state, where the sea becomes spectral and the lyric 'I' disrupts her own striking meditations – on loss, on generational memory, on departure and the resultant intermingling of selves – with sharp and plainly-spoken truths. Clearly and precisely, Fornells Nadal cuts through her constructed figurative worlds to comment on capitalism, on our punishing economy of precarious housing and long working weeks and the privilege of pursuing art. The effect is an ephemeral push and pull, where remarkable and provocative imagery makes room for its own lyric erosion. As in 'Nelumbonaceae':

> Cows. They stand there. Over the fields, power lines
> shake you, travelling
> too far backwards up to the moment where you open
> like a lotus
> that has abandoned poetry, looked at it
> from the outside, your roots
> latched in mud, submerging nightly
> into river water, reblooming sparklingly
> clean the morning after – loving – me.

Movement is also felt deeply in this collection. The poems themselves are elliptical in form; as readers, we find ourselves at multiple thresholds, crossing temporally and geographically with the speaker, as she undergoes seemingly irrevocable change, unable to tread back to what was. "Migrating" Fornells Nadal writes, in one such poem, "erased the world".

SELECTOR'S COMMENT

YOUSIF M. QASMIYEH & ALYCIA PIRMOHAMED

# ARXIPÈLAG

listen to the painter speak the only one who speaks properly and rather
      mesmerisingly, say
is it a choice to leave home and be elsewhere and
are the islands as empty as they seem, Joanna? I'd like it if they were.
      I mean I'd go there
how do you get there?
I feel guiltier eating fish, why is no one saying this? it's a disaster
the painter speaks to the head gardener but the rest of them don't listen.
      it is almost a sin
if there is sin to not care about the species there and how they survive
if I could afford to go to the island I would, and
spend time just looking around. the gardens
and the sea. spatial limitations
raise house prices by a hell of a lot
we all know well who we like to sit next to and talk to at dinner,
      although sometimes
we pretend we can change how things are

HELENA FORNELLS NADAL

# WINTER BOOK REVIEWS

With themes of travel, desire and abandon, Brechin's humorous and juicy second collection explores "explicit want" with surgeon-like precision. Reminiscent of Kim Addonizio and Diane di Prima, Brechin's poems often carve fleshy portraits of past lovers and relinquish them. Sectioned into cities that draw on Brechin's own experiences of living in Prague, Paris, Dubai and Edinburgh, *How to Make Love* offers a refreshingly brazen manifesto of modern love: a demand for lovers who'll feed you "wine straight from (their) mouth".

**HOW TO MAKE LOVE**
Annie Brechin

BLUE DIODE PRESS | £10.00 | PBS PRICE £7.50

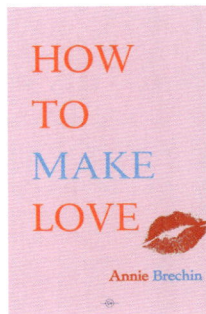

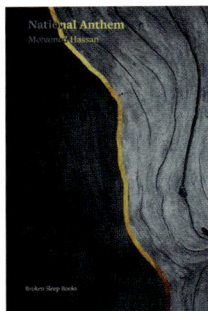

"I am not a harbinger of doom / I am just a journalist..." Mohamed Hassan doesn't shy away from what most might find repugnant and grotesque. His collection *National Anthem* is lovingly wry. He describes the humorous horror of an office party, the romance of racist airport security, the tenderness of wishing yourself dead before your loved ones. Through tongue-in-cheek titles, bodily metaphors, interesting form and visceral language, he crafts a world with his words that feels incredibly relevant.

BROKEN SLEEP BOOKS | £12.99 | PBS PRICE £9.75

In reviewing this anthology of poems by Seamus Heaney, both past and present were brought into conversation within the folds of visceral imagery that transports one "Under heaven-hue plum-blue and gorse pricked with gold". These poems are a reminder of the precious wisdom of carefully crafted words, pushing through life's mundanity yet highlighting the brilliance of the often overlooked. Heaney's approach to writing brought my soul into remembrance of this joy.

THE POEMS OF SEAMUS HEANEY

FABER | £40.00 (HB) | PBS PRICE £30.00

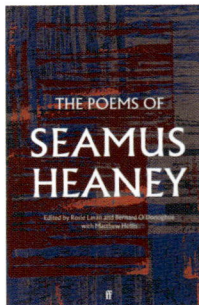

# YOUNG POETS SUMMIT

## SELIMA HILL: A MAN, A WOMAN & A HIPPOPOTAMUS
### REVIEWED BY ANZAL OMAR

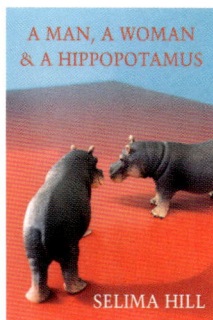

Selima Hill's *A Man, A Woman & A Hippopotamus* is wickedly funny and strange in the best way. This collection is as sharp as it is understated, transforming everyday life into a cartography of intimacy and fracture. Domestic detail collides with surreal images that feel truer than realism. Her poems expose family rifts, faith, and gendered power dynamics with biting wit in deceptively simple snapshots. The book is bold, relatable and unforgettable: a sly masterpiece of the ordinary made uncanny.

BLOODAXE BOOKS    |    £ 14.00    |    PBS PRICE £10.50

## EVAN JONES: MEN OF THE SAME NAME
### REVIEWED BY DAVID OKODEH

*Men of the Same Name* reimagines figures from myth and philosophy as present day figures. This collection echoes with philosophical questions following Jones's belief that "power and paranoia are the same thing". These poems tailor myth towards relatable dilemmas: reimagining grief, mortality and exile. The blend of short lyrical poems and detailed reimagining of myths creates a poetic dialogue which invites the reader to be immersed in the collection, skilfully showing the reader how myth is never dead, only reinterpreted.

CARCANET  PRESS    |    £12.99    |    PBS  PRICE  £9.75

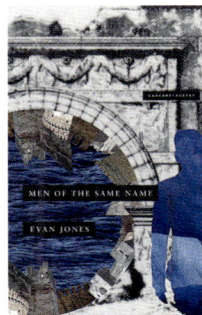

## MADELEINE KRUHLY: TO MY FATHER, NOW DEAD IN ROOM 318
### REVIEWED BY SETH CONNOR-FULLWOOD

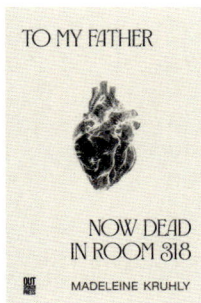

Most of the poems in *To My Father, Now Dead in Room 318*, a very strong debut, fit on a single page; a handful take two. The collection becomes a series of vignettes, connected by the recurring images throughout. The way Kruhly plays with the layout of her poetry is very interesting. Her intriguing, arresting imagery creates a dreamlike atmosphere. Equally, the contrasting more plainly emotional moments, such as the end of 'One', are memorable highlights.

OUT-SPOKEN  PRESS    |    £11.99    |    PBS  PRICE  £9.00

BOOK REVIEWS

Megan Pinto's stunning debut interrogates South Asian experiences of religion, domestic violence, and addiction with devastating intimacy. Pinto's language is unflinching, where a fluctuating retrospective of adolescence brims with life: "Obsession is a godless place. I go there every day." Elsewhere, Pinto deftly excavates the emotional labour that accompanies different types of love, portraying grief in a simultaneously visceral and tender light. These aren't simply poems, they're movies with confessions, snowscapes, and stars lost to space.

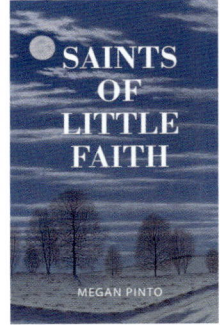

THE 87 PRESS    |    £16.99    |    PBS PRICE £12.75

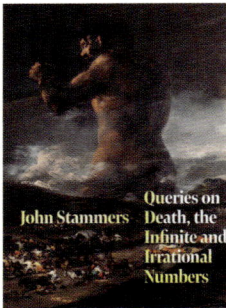

Stammers's collection offers a brilliant meditation on death, memory, and focus. The phrase "life had not finished with me yet; there was some more of it" lingers at thresholds where perception outlives the body. Voices from the past and present weave together to reclaim myth, friendship, and childhood. Insisting that "to be truly of the world is to care for it for the right reasons", Stammers's sensuous accuracy honours the world above all else, from pigeons at dusk to the "golden wheatfield" fur of a leveret.

PICADOR    |    £12.99    |    PBS PRICE £9.75

*Magadh* traces vanished kingdoms and India's historical and mythic past in spare poems that circle, insistently, around repetitions and riddling questions; history is rendered less as narrative than as an atmosphere heavy with absence. Rahul Soni's translation carries this stark power with clarity and restraint. The work feels both ancient and urgently present, just as Verma's retrospective ubi sunt draws us to consider our own situation within cycles of rise and decline. A remarkable, disorienting book that resists closure or consolation.

AND OTHER STORIES    |    £14.99    |    PBS PRICE £11.25

**Magadh**
*Shrikant Verma*

&

¶ Listen horseman. where's Maga-dh? ¶ I've come ¶ from Maga-dh ¶ I must go to ¶ Magadh¶ ¶ Where ¶ do I turn?¶ North or south. ¶ east or west? ¶ ¶ Here I see Magadh. ¶ here it disappears...
*Translated by Rahul Soni*

## LAURA WAINWRIGHT: THE STORM'S FLORA
### REVIEWED BY CHARLOTTE MURRAY

This collection explores different kinds of storms: cultural, political, artistic and climatic. Firmly rooted in Welsh history and landscape, ancient stories are rewritten in new and surprising ways, weaving together art, song, folklore, memory and the psyche. As we wild swim through the musicality of the poems, we are constantly reminded of forces greater than ourselves – "and over us, dark gold, the gorse aurora" – a world where nature has its own intentions, but also one under threat from humanity's destructive impulses.

SEREN | £10.99 | PBS PRICE £8.25

## ANTOSH WOJCIK: SUBURBAN LOCUST
### REVIEWED BY EVA LEWIS

Ecological disasters, family dynamics, addiction, migration and trauma share a porous membrane in Wojcik's surreal, topographic poems. Interconnected, as though dormant genes are gradually activated, the book shares the cyclical, echolalic pattern of time. Artificial-natural and past-present are assimilated and repressed memory threatens dehumanisation: "dad seals the front door, requesting we leave via cat flap". This darkly witty collection lodges in your body like a family curse.

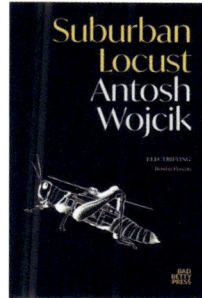

BAD BETTY PRESS | £10.99 | PBS PRICE £8.25

## EMILY ZOBEL MARSHALL: OTHER WILD
### REVIEWED BY ALEXIA McPHERSON

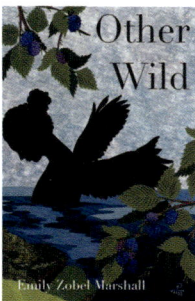

*Other Wild* explores the landscape of lives, weaving natural metaphor, memory, Welsh, French-Caribbean history and myth to confront love, loss, power, and family. Marshall's poignant use of form exposes the irrefutable connection of humanity and nature; the never-ending cycle of life and death. Political commentary, carefully crafted, focuses on her own cultures, and longing for authenticity which can sometimes only be found in the wilderness: "I see that my cwm is embraced / by the mountains that know me".

PEEPAL TREE PRESS | £10.99 | PBS PRICE £8.25

BOOK REVIEWS

# THE WRITING SQUAD

## LEWIS BUXTON: MATE ARIAS
### REVIEWED BY MEGAN ROBSON

This bright and tender pamphlet from Lewis Buxton further explores the subject of modern masculinity which shaped his debut collection, *Boy in Various Poses*, connecting it with themes of love and friendship. Comprising twenty-three subtly crafted sonnets, punctuated with wit, joy, and warmth, *Mate Arias* sings into the silences which surround male emotions. As the second sonnet 'Alright mate?' puts it: "what an unexpected cup of tea, / what a slow rainbow" this fine little volume is.

**Mate Arias**

Poems by
Lewis Buxton

THE EMMA PRESS                              £7.99

## JO MORRIS DIXON: STRAWBERRIES
### REVIEWED BY GREGORY KEARNS

Strawberries
Jo Morris Dixon

Broken Sleep Books

Jo Morris Dixon's *Strawberries* explores the paradox of therapising language, how it can bring validation to our pain, but it can also be used to alienate and decontextualise our experiences. *Strawberries* also calls us to hope, not as a wish or a negation of fear and grief, but as an affirmation of life, including all its difficult shades. These humorous and tender poems remind us that "being alive means we need to try harder".

BROKEN SLEEP BOOKS                          £9.99

## REMI GRAVES: COAL
### REVIEWED BY KAYLEIGH JAYSHREE

"If gender be a place (…) let me be unfindable there" Remi Graves's speaker declares in 'On Bilocation'. This pamphlet renews the story of Paul Downing, using photography, fragments, illustration and records to draw parallels across time and space, where Paul's voice acts as an echoing howl, a shadow drawn across the world. Remi Graves uses their position as a poet to act as a mouth, a portal, a map.

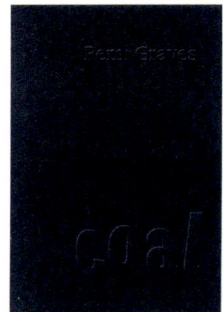

Remi Graves

coal

MONITOR BOOKS                              £14.00